THE HAND OF GOD

Epistle of Christ
(2 Corinthians 3:3)

Charles G. Woods

CROSSBOOKS

CrossBooks™
A Division of LifeWay
1663 Liberty Drive
Bloomington, IN 47403
www.crossbooks.com
Phone: 1-866-879-0502

First published by CrossBooks 5/03/2012

ISBN: 978-1-4627-1696-8 (sc)
ISBN: 978-1-4627-1695-1 (e)

Library of Congress Control Number: 2012907180

Printed in the United States of America

This book is printed on acid-free paper.

Dedicated to

My Lord and Savior Jesus Christ,

and

Joanne,
Who has steadfastly remained at my side,
believed in me, and loved me.
She is my love, my life, and my inspiration.
She was a gift from God, and
I am blessed to have her in my life.
"One life, One wife."

Contents

Acknowledgments

This book was written by the author at the behest of God Almighty but could not have been completed in book form without the unselfish talents of the following members of the author's family.

Jill, my daughter-in-law, who took time out from her very busy schedule as a devoted mom to my three precious granddaughters and from her job as a school administrator.

Rick, my brother-in-law, who owns and operates a printing company and whose generosity is second to none. His staff helped bring this book to life through their artistic abilities.

Matt, my son; Audra, my daughter; Zack and Chadd, my grandsons; and Molly, Abby, and Reilly, my granddaughters, have all painstakingly stood by me and believed in me throughout my many life-changing experiences. Without their love and unfailing support, I am certain I would not be where I am today.

Joanne, my beloved wife, is my all. Without her, there would be no me.

Charles R. Swindoll is, in my opinion, one of the best Christian writers of our time. His books inspired me in a way none others have. His book *David: A Man of Passion and Destiny* is so well written it inspired me to read the rest of the books in his series exploring great lives from the Bible.

and

God the Father, Jesus Christ, and the Holy Spirit … without this Holy Trinity, I would have been lost to darkness long ago. Everything I have, everything good in my life, and who I am today are blessings bestowed on me by my Father in Heaven through His Son, Jesus Christ.

Christianity is truth. Truth is knowledge, and through knowledge we have faith. Through faith we are saved by Grace. *Sola scriptura, sola gratia,* and *sola fide*—Scripture alone, Grace alone, and faith alone. I am a Christian, and I believe in and strive to live by these three doctrines.

In His service
"tishimself"

Introduction

Over the years, it has come to my attention that the best place to begin is at the beginning. Thusly, I shall endeavor to bring to all who have been led to this book about my life—bumps and all—a work that inspires. I have never written a book before, so I have no clue how to do it. Be that as it may, God has His plan. I apparently have been recruited by God to spread the Gospel in this manner. God is leading me to do this, and He is not of a mind to debate the matter. So here I am, at sixty-three years of age, handicapped, writing about my life. I can tell you this: my life has not been dull. Peace be with you all. Welcome to my world.

In His Service,

"tishimself"

Even a child is known by his doings, whether his work be pure, whether it be right.

Proverbs 20:11 KJV

Chapter 1
The Beginning

I was brought into this world in 1948, the first of three sons born to my parents. My childhood was great. We enjoyed a moderate lifestyle, somewhere between not having much and having just enough.

My dad was a big Irish-German cop, and mom Mom raised us boys. I grew up in a neighborhood full of boys, somewhere between the Bowery Boys and the Dead End Kids. We grew up full of mischief—the kind you might see in the movie *West Side Story*. I was a skinny kid with a passion for running everywhere I went. I ran because I always needed to be on time, and it was a good way to stay a few steps ahead of the local bullies. Oh yes, bullies are a way of life for most kids growing up. (I dislike bullies to this day.) In fact, my first introduction to physical violence occurred when I was about five years old. While I was playing outside, an older boy took his pocketknife and slashed my face. Welcome to the neighborhood, kid. Now, I had known fear in my young life. Of course, there were monster movies at the local theater. Every town had a theater in those days that showed a double-feature horror show with five cartoons between movies. Scary movies, though, were no comparison to my dad. My dad had a look when he was displeased that would cause a goat to pass out from his stare. It was almost diabolical. It scared me, in any event.

Back to my introduction to physical violence. We played all day, and baseball was our game. I was involved in such an activity one summer day. I was at home plate, ready to take a swing at the old calfskin. However, the pitcher, who was about nine years old, threw wild and hit me (not uncommon in such pick-up games). It hurt, I sniveled, and the catcher, a bully I knew well, laughed harder than he needed to. He pushed me, picked on me, and bullied me. I got angry and boldly stated, "I quit, and I'm taking my bat and ball home." Well, that wasn't going to happen, as the bully pointed out to me. I showed him; I left my bat and ball and smartly marched off the field and ran home in tears. It was then my dad gave me my first serious "life lesson." My dad never conversed with me; he yelled at me, got angry at me, gave me his "look," or occasionally gave me a whack or two with his two-inch-wide police belt. Don't get excited; it was not abuse. It hurt, yes, but I always deserved it, and I never hated Dad for it. But I digress (I do this a lot). Back to my lesson. As I entered our kitchen, looking for Mom—who would pacify me with hugs, milk, and cookies—I found Dad sitting at the kitchen table. Oh no! I stopped in my tracks, still sniveling, and tears running down my face. My dad: the last person on earth who I wanted to see me crying. But there he was, his look directed at me, all six feet four inches and 280 pounds of Irish-German cop. Life as I knew it was about to change forever. He demanded, in a voice I was sure he used on criminals like murderers and rapists, to know why I was crying. I had to tell him. I didn't dare lie to my dad, so the truth spilled out of me through sobs. "Stop whining!" he demanded. "Stand up straight!" (Did you ever notice as a kid you were always being told to stand up straight or sit up straight?) He then, with directness, explained to me exactly what I was going to do. It was not a suggestion; it was a commandment, an order that had to be carried out. Of this I had no doubt. It is now that I should explain that behaviors such as forgiving your enemies, turning the other cheek, and loving your neighbor were not practiced by my dad, and thus were not learned by me. I was not familiar with God, religion, or the Bible. Jesus was the guy who had a birthday on December 25 of each year, and I got presents. That's what I knew. Church was something we did on rare occasions: weddings, funerals, a couple times with friends. Religion was not alive or well in our home as I grew up.

So, with my dad's command ringing in my ears that I was to return to that baseball field and get my bat and ball back any way I had to, off I went. I was to "knock the bully on his ass," and if I ever came home crying again, he (my dad) would give me something to cry about. I believed everything Dad said. I feared him. I respected him. A bit of a contradiction of terms I think. However, I think fear and respect are feelings that are interchangeable. I feared my dad's disappointment in me, yet I respected his strength as a man—his character—yet these things made me cautious of him.

So, with all my fears (and I feared my dad more than anything the bully could do to me), I marched with determination, conviction, and fear back to the baseball field. I walked directly up to the bully. He took off his catcher's mask and made a degrading remark to me, and in that moment, in the blink of an eye, my life changed forever. I punched him. I hit him in his eye so hard I surprised myself. He went down. The look on his face was pure shock. He never bullied me again. I felt exhilarated, I felt powerful, I felt strong for the first time in my life, and I was glad. My dad was proud, I was proud, and I went forth into my world eliminating bullies, walking tall. And my life became one of confrontation and violence. I became good at it, and I thrived on it.

However, it was not what I wanted. It was not who I really was. I had a soft, sensitive side I rarely displayed. I feared being seen as weak, a target, a boy bullies could hurt. As a child, I was conflicted between that scared boy and my newfound power as a guy to be reckoned with. So I concealed the boy who cared. I let no one see me cry at movies like *Old Yeller* or *The Yearling*. No one but my mom knew that at the age of eleven, I would go to our neighborhood hospital's children's ward and play with sick children; I would even take them some of my toys as gifts. I would get them to laugh and got some who had refused to eat to do so. I had a heart for children and still do. I now know this is a blessing from God.

Behold, I stand at the door, and knock: If any man hear my voice, and open the door, I will come in to him, and will sup with him and he with me."

Revelation 3:20 KJV

Do not be misled:
Bad company corrupts good character.

I Corinthians 15:33 KJV

Chapter II
My Formative Years

Formative years: the years of shaping, setting a way of doing or saying something, and a time when my behavior or performance was set with respect to expectations, morals, obligations, ethics, and faith. Oh, I beg to differ. I was a teenager. I knew it all. Rock 'n' roll was king. Besides, I was becoming a force to be feared in my world. Fighting, beer, and girls (not necessarily in that order) were the norm in the 1960s. School: I loved it and got kicked out of it a number of times for fighting. I mean, "High school days have some delights, but can't compare to those high school nights." For me, the ninth through the twelfth grades were one big party. I learned little from my teachers but a whole lot from the streets. I was well on my way to being a really proficient sinner.

You may be wondering where God was in all this. What about religion? Well, God and religion didn't figure into it. I knew more about beer than I did about religion. Besides, those Holy Roller people were odd, to say the least. Does "Blind and cannot see, and deaf and cannot hear" come to mind? So it was without faith in anything more than my fists that I went through my formative teenage years.

Now, having said all this, I need to let it be known that I might not have given a single thought to God during my formative years, but that doesn't mean He wasn't there. He is always there; the morally blind and ethically deaf just don't see or hear Him. God, the Holy Spirit, and Jesus reach out to us throughout our lives. They knock. We need only to open the door and let them in.

In my senior year of high school, I had an experience that would affect me the rest of my life. I was happily sinning my way through life. Then one night, some friends and I were involved in a horrendous car wreck. We had been drinking, of course. It was late, and one poor decision on our part led to another, and we ended up in a deep ditch on a desolate rural road. We hit a cement bridge abutment. I was in the front passenger seat and was thrown into the windshield. I awoke to find steam and smoke boiling out the front of what was left of the car. My three companions were unconscious. I was bleeding from head wounds and paralyzed from the waist down. (I would later find out it was caused by the dislocation of my right hip.) Oddly enough, I was not scared: perhaps because I was drinking; maybe because I was a macho tough guy. Whatever the reason, I was calm.

I evaluated my situation and felt a need to exit the car. Did I mention I was paralyzed from my waist down and more or less trapped where I was? In spite of all this, I pulled myself through the side window: no easy feat for a six-foot-two, 210-pound middle linebacker with a shoulder width of about fifty-six inches. I went through a small window on a small car without the aid of my legs. I dropped with a splash into the ditch. The water was about a foot deep, and I landed facedown against the side of the car. I realized I couldn't move, and my hands were covered with mud. I felt my arms slowly sink deeper into the mud. The mud held tightly, with a suction that was a wee bit unnerving. My face got closer to the water every time I struggled to pull out one of my arms. Oh yes, when doing so, my other arm sank deeper. And so it went, until my face was resting in water, and I realized I was about to drown. Surprisingly, I still was not panicked or frightened, even though I strained to keep my head above water.

What happened next is a blessing: God knocked, spoke to me, or came to my rescue with divine intervention, however you want to say it, believe it, or whatever words can be used to describe it. I answered Him. God came unto me, a nonbeliever, and I followed Him. He spoke, and I listened. He intervened, and I paid attention. By His grace, I was blessed and about to be saved. Just before my strength gave out and my head was to go underwater, I took notice of a serene silence that came upon me. The sounds of frogs, crickets, and insects ceased, and a solemn peace came over me. I suddenly felt myself pulling my arms out of the sucking, thick mud.

I began crawling, pulling myself up the steep bank with my fingers, and dragging my legs behind me. When I found myself out of the water and safe from drowning, I felt a presence and the need to look up at the top of the ditch. In the beautiful silence that was about me, I saw an arch of translucent, soft, white light surrounding three tall angels. There was an angel in the center, and one on either side and slightly lower than the one in the center. The gowns they wore were also translucent white, draped elegantly from their neck to the ground. All three had a golden halo about their heads and large pure white wings folded neatly behind them and rising a few inches above their shoulders. But what was most striking to me was that not one of the angels had a face. They were void of any identifiable facial features. What was there was a fleshy, light pink color but no eyes, nose, or mouth. They were silent. I was compelled to crawl toward them, and once again, using my fingers like claws, I began crawling up the ditch toward them. I felt warm and secure in their presence. I was unafraid with a need to be closer to them. As I reached the ditch apex, I turned my face upward to see them. They were gone, and the silence was replaced by the night sounds of frogs croaking, crickets chirping, and insects buzzing. It was only then that I could hear the sounds of sirens getting closer. I was transported to a nearby hospital, where I spent several days recovering from my injuries, including a dislocated right hip. My friends were also hospitalized but were not seriously injured.

I never spoke of the angels to anyone; I was certain people would think I was crazy or stone drunk. Neither was true, but I remained silent until several years later, when I was working as a police officer and became friends with a Catholic priest who was our police chaplain. I had still not accepted Jesus at this point, being a police officer, I mean. I still had Vietnam and much more to go through before I would become a born-again Christian.

A society is only as good as
its religious doctrine influences the family.

tishimself

Chapter III

One Life, One Wife

It was during the end of my senior year—while being wild, reckless, and on a path destined to lead me into an abyss—that I met my future wife, Joanne. She would prove not only to be a blessing from God but the love of my life.

Only God could have brought us together. We were total opposites. She was slight of build; had long, dark brown hair; and olive skin. She wore dresses, no makeup you could see, and she was shy almost to a fault. I, on the other hand, was the personification of "the good, the bad, and the ugly." Mostly the big, the bad, and the ugly. My theme song back then would have been, "I Fought the Law, and the Law Won," or "What You Going to Do When They Come for you, Bad Boy, Bad Boy." Of course, I didn't see myself as that bad. I admit I drank beer, got in lots of fights (remember the bullies), and was not the best student. I did, however, have some morals and ethics, and I was sensitive. I just didn't show it, because

I saw it as a weakness that could be exploited and used against me.

You can see why Joanne totally ignored my advances. But not to be put off, I persisted. She continued to ignore me, and "himself" (that would be me), who is not so easily ignored, had a plan. One day at school, I saw her coming down the hall toward me. I not so nonchalantly gave her a shoulder bump, causing her to drop her books. I leaped into action, apologizing up one side and down the other as I helped her pick up her books. Well, I can't for the life of me explain why, but she agreed to go out with me. God blessed our union together, and we have been married forty-three years. She is my life, my everything, and when I accepted Christ as my personal savior years later, I knew when, where, how, and why He blessed us that day in 1966 in a hallway at our high school.

Greater love has no one than this,
that he lay down his life for his friends.
John 15:13 NKJV

I have fought the good fight
I have finished the race
I have kept the faith.
2 Timothy 4:7 NIV

Chapter IV

My Year in Vietnam

"Good morning, Vietnam." The good news is I graduated from high school. The not so good news was I was thirteen thousand miles from home and getting shot at. It was April 1968, and I was serving as a machine gunner in a mechanized RECON unit with the 1st Infantry Division. And just for the record, I enlisted in the US Army; they didn't have to draft me. I was ready and willing to go fight for my country. After all, I was good at fighting. Fear was like a drug for me that I found heightened my ability to accomplish the task at hand: rendering my opponents helpless, if not worse. I was, as a black soldier in my unit noted, an "action junkie."

I thrived on the action; danger made me very alert, and violence put me on the edge. I went toward the sound of gunfire, not away from it. When my senses were at such a heightened state, I was, in fact, dangerous, and I knew it. I believed no one and no thing were better than my weapons and I. God was never a part of my thought process. I trusted me and me alone.

Having said this, I will tell you God was alive, well, and in Vietnam with me, watching over me and keeping me from harm's way. Of course, I didn't know this, because my ego and I were taking all the credit and praising "dumb luck" for keeping me alive. You know, there is something to be learned about God loving sinners and fools, and Lord knows I walked the walk and talked the talk of the sinner and the fool. I came very near death several times in Vietnam, but God always blessed me. I eluded death, which was nothing short of miraculous.

Things then got really interesting, but it wasn't until years later, when I became a born-again Christian, that I knew it was God—not me—who was in charge and that His divine intervention in my life was why I miraculously survived the infamous Tet Offensive of 1968, which was the Vietnamese New Year. I survived living in the Iron Triangle, one of the areas of Vietnam most heavily sprayed with Agent Orange. Did I come out of Vietnam unscathed? No, I did not. I was wounded and awarded the Purple Heart Medal. But not all wounds are visible. I suffer from post traumatic stress disorder (PTSD). War, death, violence, cruelty, and innocence lost never leaves your psyche. It scars your soul. Sin scars our souls. My soul has many scars. So many scars, and no faith, no religion, no Jesus in my life. It is certainly a recipe for self-destruction; a perfect condition for evil to take hold of your soul. I knew nothing of such things, and like a bull in a China shop, I went forward, one dangerous, violent, hateful incident after another. The good, the bad, the ugly that was Vietnam. Lots of bad and ugly, and not so much good.

One such good time (more sad for me than good) was Christmas Eve 1967. I was drinking beer in the Enlisted Men's Club (EM Club) at our base camp in Lai Khe, Vietnam. I was one of three soldiers in the club. It was late in the afternoon, and rumor had it that "Charlie" (the Viet Cong) was planning an all-out massive attack against us, since it was Christmas and all. Anyway, in the door comes this lieutenant, who says he needs volunteers for all-night sentry duty on our perimeter due to the imminent VC (Viet Cong) attacks. He pointed at the three of us, declared us volunteers, and ordered us to gear up. He dropped each of us off at a remote spot on the perimeter, overlooking a kill zone known as "no man's land." The bunker fortification I was assigned to had two soldiers already in it. These two guys were buddies, but I didn't know either one of them. We greeted each other, and I set up my weapons and settled in. As darkness fell, my bunker mates decided it was time to light up a couple marijuana joints. They were generous guys and offered me one, which I declined. First of all, I wasn't into dope, and second, if the VC attacked, I wanted to be alert and at the top of my game.

As the night passed, all I could hear was the sounds of frogs, insects, small animals, and the nonsensical ramblings of the two knuckleheads I got stuck with:

Tweedle Dee and Tweedle Dum. They were very high, having consumed more marijuana than necessary. They were in no condition to fight and were a threat to my safety. (Thus again confirming why I trusted no one.) I was not pleased with my situation or my companions.

Along about midnight, both of those clowns finally passed out. I was relieved, because they were no longer loud and lighting their Zippos, pinpointing our position. The thought of smothering them momentarily crossed my mind. As I sat there, with them passed out, a peaceful serenity came over me, much like what occurred after the auto accident in high school. The calm caused me to notice the sounds of the frogs, insects, and the night had gone silent, but I could faintly hear something behind me in the distant darkness. At first, I couldn't quite make it out, though it was a familiar sound. In the dark, lonely bunker, I strained to identify the sound. I wasn't alarmed. I was calm and at peace as the sound got just loud enough so I could identify it. It was the masculine voices of soldiers back in the center of the base camp, probably at the EM Club. They were singing "Silent Night," and it sounded in perfect harmony. They could have been the Vienna Boys Choir from the beautiful singing I heard. It was truly a group of soldiers "making a joyful noise" at midnight on Christmas Eve 1967. I was overwhelmed with emotion, the likes of which I had not experienced since I was a boy and wept at the movies when Old Yeller was killed. I never let anyone see my tears back then. After all, I was taught boys never cried; only girls cried. As I listened to the beauty of the words to "Silent Night" as they came more clearly, I felt the tears stream down my face. At that moment in time, and to this day, I have never felt so lonely and never appreciated a song more. When the song ended, there were no more, and the sounds of the night returned. I kept my watch and survived another night in Vietnam, having received a blessing from God that I would not appreciate until many years later.

So went my tour of duty in Vietnam. Any number of incidents can only be explained by faith and the knowledge that there is a God who watches over the faithful, the weak, the sinners, and fools. I was no hero in Vietnam or during my twenty-year tenure as a police officer and public safety officer. I served; I was a warrior and patriot. I had an unexplainable desire and need to protect those who could not protect themselves—the old, the kids, the weak. I just thought it was me, and that's the way things were. I was tough and strong, good at confrontation and fighting. Again, God never entered into the workings of my mind.

We were subjected to three months worth of bombardment during the Tet Offensive. Once when I was in my hooch (hut), a soldier who was just a couple days "in country" was lying on his rack (bed) next to me. It was the middle of the night when enemy bombardment came. Suddenly, there were loud explosions of rockets and mortar fire, huge flashes of light, and loud crashing and yelling as soldiers ran for cover. Too late for me and the new guy. Everywhere around our hooch was exploding. Pandemonium surrounded us! I dropped to the floor, pulling my mattress on top of me, affording what protection it could. I could hear the new guy, screaming hysterically next to me. I looked out from under the cover of my mattress to see him running in a circle, screaming, eyes wild and wide, and a look of sheer terror on his face. I yelled at him several times, "Get down, take cover!" But he couldn't hear me over his own screams and the roar of the rounds exploding all around us. I was compelled to do something, Otherwise "new guy" would become "dead guy." I left the cover of my mattress, got up, and grabbed hold of him as he ran by me, still screaming. He began to fight me and would not listen. I slapped his face, and he went limp, his eyes wide with surprise. I pulled him to the ground and covered him with his mattress. I sternly told him, "Stay there!" I could hear him sobbing, and he did not stop until it was over. We got to our feet in due time, and he said nothing. He was ashamed and walked away, his head hung low. I never saw him again. I, on the other hand, felt nothing—just another night I survived in Vietnam—numb to what I had lived through but alive. I lived through so many situations—experienced so much hostility, destruction, violence, and death—I found it difficult to determine good from bad, truth from lies, or right from wrong.

Many of my "on death's doorstep" close encounters in 'Nam came at the hands of other American soldiers. That's right, it wasn't "All for one, and one for all.'" It got real scary at times, GI against GI, and sometimes guys died. I nearly lost my life one night when a Vietnamese boy led another soldier and I through a wire into a village. As we approached a hooch (a typical Vietnamese home) in the dark, two hand grenades were thrown at us. We heard them thump to the ground, and we dove for cover. Both grenades exploded. Then there was yelling, crying, and panic. The boy who led us into the village appeared, yelling in broken English, "Mamasan hurt, you help!" We were only several feet from the door of the hooch. The boy led us inside, where sprawled on the dirt floor was an old lady, bleeding profusely. She was on her back, not breathing, so the guy I was with began CPR on her. As he blew into her mouth, he told me to do chest compressions. I told him I didn't know CPR. He gave me a quick how-to lesson, and I took over. A couple minutes later, the boy kneeled next to me. I asked where the VC who had thrown the grenades were. He responded, "No VC, no VC. Black brothers threw grenades at you." I asked if he meant black American soldiers. He said, "Yes, black GIs." I asked if he knew why. He replied, "Black GIs were AWOL[absent without leave], living in the village, and thought you were MPs [military police]." I again asked him where they were. He told me they ran away. I was still doing chest compressions on the old Vietnamese lady (for all the good it did; she was dead), when all of a sudden, the hooch door came crashing in. I found myself looking directly into the muzzle of an AK-47 assault rifle. Holding the rifle was a shirtless Vietnamese soldier, wearing tiger camouflage pants and yelling in

Vietnamese. At that moment, I was certain I was about to die. Within a few seconds, two American MPs came through the door and took charge. The guy holding the AK to my head was an ARVN (he was on our side) soldier home on leave.

Bing, bang, boom, we found ourselves under arrest and transported to the M.P. office. We told our story and put it in writing. We told them about the boy and the black soldiers who threw the grenades at us. We were sent back to our unit pending an investigation regarding the death of a civilian. Within two days, we were informed we would not be charged with anything, as the old woman was killed by a "short round," possibly friendly fire. Case closed. They never did acknowledge that two black soldiers killed the old lady and tried to kill us—all while hiding out in the village because they were AWOL from their unit. Hard to believe, isn't it? Or perhaps I made up the black soldiers. Well, anything's possible in Vietnam. Yes, I survived another night in Vietnam. By the way, those were the only black guys in Vietnam who tried to zap me (word used by soldiers inplace of kill). However, white soldiers tried twice to kill me.

I was again in a village at night, when a Vietnamese woman led me to a locked hooch. She unlocked the padlock on the door and fled as I pushed the door in and entered the very dark room. Night vision inside the hooch was zero. As I stepped into the room, a gun was placed to the right side of my head, and I heard the unmistakable click of the hammer on a Model 1911 45-pistol. Take my word for it, you never forget that sound! I froze dead in my tracks, and an American voice said, "If you're an MP, I'm going to blow your brains out!"

Needless to say, I was extremely happy at that moment that I was not an MP. I spoke as confidently as I could. "I'm not an MP. Don't kill me!"

At that point, a second American voice said, "Put the gun down. He's not an MP," and the gun was removed from my head. One asked, "Who are you? Why you here? What's up? What's new?" as my sphincter muscle unwound from the choke hold it had tightened into. One of the guys popped open his Zippo lighter and illuminated the small room. The guy with the lighter was an army buck sergeant E-5, and the other guy was a second lieutenant. Both were dressed in their khaki uniforms. They informed me they were not returning to their units up north. They were buddies and had gone on R&R (rest and relaxation) to Thailand and were hiding out in the village from the MPs. They told me they couldn't take combat anymore and weren't going back. After exchanging pleasantries with these two guys, I excused myself and got out of there. I never saw them again. I survived yet another "fun-filled" night in 'Nam.

Now you're probably thinking, *Enough of Vietnam already!* Well, I'm sorry, but this is very therapeutic for a guy who has PTSD. Not to mention these incidents had a direct impact on my future entry into Christianity. I mean, read between the lines. On April 2, 1968, 364 days and a wake up, I returned to the world: the good old United States of America and my neighborhood. "It wasn't but a thang!" (Slang saying used by soldiers in Vietnam.)

*You gain strength, courage, and confidence every time
you look fear in the face.*

Eleanor Roosevelt

*I therefore … beseech you that ye walk worthy of the vocation
wherewith ye are called.*

Ephesians 4:1 NKJV

*For we wrestle not against flesh and blood, but
against principalities, against powers, against
the rulers of darkness of the world,
against spiritual wickedness in high places.
Wherefore take unto you the whole armour of God,
that you may be able to withstand in evil day,
and having done all to stand.*

Ephesians 6:12–13 NIV

Chapter V

In the Shadow of the Beast

Go figure. I survived Vietnam, the Tet Offensive, Agent Orange, and several near misses on my life. I was back in my own bed on April 4, 1968, surrounded by family. Notice I said family, not friends. Most of my running buddies from high school were in the military, in Vietnam, or away at school. The few still hanging around the neighborhood didn't know I had gone anywhere, let alone been to Vietnam. It was surreal, like I had never gone away. Just a side note, we were not treated very well by the public on our return. Enough said about that.

So I'm home on the fourth and married Joanne on April 20, 1968. It was a big, Catholic, Polish wedding in Joanne's home parish; a full mass no less. Now here is where you might be wondering how I got into the church. Well, it wasn't easy, but looking back on it as a Christian, I can tell you that God's hand was in it. "Blessed again" comes to mind. See, Joanne's church refused to marry us, mostly because I was not Catholic, and the word "heathen" comes to mind. In all fairness, that's not too far from the truth. But it was very important to Joanne and her family that we be married in the eyes of God in her home church. "Okay, sure, yeah, not a problem," I said. "What do I have to do?" Well, I had to become a Catholic. I'm in 'Nam—hello! But there is no obstacle God cannot overcome. With a lot of prayer from Joanne and a call here and letter there, lo and behold, I learn that I can get instructions and get baptized, the whole nine yards, right in Vietnam—if the brigade chaplain (who happens to be a priest; am I a lucky guy or what?) agreed to do what was necessary and proper to allow me to wed my high school sweetheart in her home church. He agreed.

Things just come together when God is involved. Of course, I didn't understand any of it. I didn't care—church, no church, whatever. The brigade chaplain agreed to give me classes, and I did what I was told. I found another GI to be my godfather, and after a few days of instruction in a blown-up shell of a church, I was baptized into the Catholic Church. And all was well with the world. Happily married we became, and we still are, forty-three years later. And so, something good came out of Vietnam.

I settled into married life, but the violence and hostility were still with me. I dealt with it like I had always done: head-on, fists clenched. This scared Joanne, I'm sure, but she knew she was safe with me. I decided to become a police officer and, in 1969, left the army and joined my hometown police force. What a twenty-year ride I had! Not enough ink, paper, or time to tell it all. I will relate incidents that had significant meaning as it pertains to my search for the truth that ultimately led me to Christianity. Now, if you think the chapter on Vietnam was something, you haven't heard anything yet.

Police work in 1969 through the mid-1980s was wild. Drugs, war protesters, biker gangs, racial problems: it was much to my liking. It was like being back in Vietnam except I got to go home to Joanne at night. Well, most of the time. You will see my road trip into degeneration would lead me deeper into sin, and I was comfortable there, cautious and watchful, but comfortable. After all, one year in Vietnam was like five years on the street in and around my stomping grounds. I experienced the beast and he was real. On at least four occasions, I came face to face with evil in human form—its eyes dead and black as coal—and I knew real fear. I was being swallowed up, sinking deeper into the slime that is hell on earth. But let's not get too far ahead of the story.

I was eager and hopeful when I put on the badge. I was married, had a good job, and was working with men of integrity and grit; or so I thought. It only took me a year to realize the bonding I hoped for among "brother officers" didn't exist, no more than it had in Vietnam. Yes, there were close friendships between partners, a bonding many wives could not understand or deal with. But those were exceptions, not the rule. It was truly "a thin blue line." None of this was a big surprise to me, It was a disappointment for sure, but as a loner for many years, trusting no one, I kept on trucking, doing my thing. I was very good at doing my thing. I looked high and low, in and out of every alley, parking lot, and roadway for "bad guys," and I found them. It was easy for me; I was at the top of my game. The highs I got from the job drove me, and at the end of an action–filled shift, I went out drinking to unwind and relive the action. (I truly was an action junkie.) I was in love with the job, the street, the action, and the high it gave me. It was my mistress: an extension of Vietnam. It was what I was, not what I did. It was not a job to me, and it came first in my life. It never stopped until my career ended twenty years later in a high-speed chase that nearly took my life and left me crippled. I don't have a clue how Joanne put up with it. (See God's hand at work here?) In any event, suffice it to say I was, in three words, "out of control."

One of my brothers came back from Vietnam, got out of the US Marine Corps, joined a larger, neighboring police department. He worked undercover most of his career and several years in vice and morality. Hookers, pimps, lowlifes—you name it. We ran together. Go-go bars were our watering holes of choice, and motorcycles our choice of rides. You can only imagine what we wallowed in and out of. Neon slime night in and night out.

During these first years on the job, Joanne and I were blessed with a son. We were living in a small apartment at the time. I was working midnights (graveyard shift) and loving it. There was lots of fast and furious action. The baby was healthy and doing well. I had it all going on, but something happened on a cold February night in 1970 that started me down a path that would once again significantly affect my life forever.

I was at work. I most often worked alone; I liked it that way. I had made an arrest some time after midnight and was in our squad room, processing my prisoner. We worked out of a public safety facility that included our firefighters. The fire guys ran an ambulance service out of the facility. A firefighter was also the city dispatcher while other firemen slept. Anyway, a broadcast was sent out over our intercom, waking up the sleeping firemen. The dispatcher informed the crew they had a baby who had stopped breathing, and he gave out the address. To my horror, it was my address! I immediately responded to my home, getting there before the ambulance. I pulled up in front of my apartment. Joanne, in her nightgown, stood at the open door, holding our son out in front of her. Joanne could not speak; she could not respond to my questions. Her face was pure white and her eyes were blank and staring past me; she was in shock. My son was completely blue and not breathing at all. I took him from Joanne and ran the few yards to my squad car. I could hear the siren of the ambulance in the distance. It was not going to get there in time. Panic rose inside of me. I had no idea what to do. I was not trained in CPR, let alone infant CPR. Oh sure, I had heard about it at the police academy, but I had not attempted it since Vietnam. Now here's where things take a divine turn. I had never followed a religion or evoked the name of God or Jesus or anyone else. I was a sinner, a nonbeliever, a pagan if you will, so no one was more surprised than I by what occurred next. It was cold, very cold. It was early February, and there was snow on the ground. The late night sky was full of bright stars. A sudden, familiar silence and peace came upon me. It was a silence and peace I had experienced twice before: in the car wreck in the ditch and in Vietnam on Christmas Eve 1967.

I became very calm and lifted my infant son high over my head toward the night sky. I pleaded, "God, please, no!" In that moment of desperation, in the twinkling of an eye, I knew exactly what I must do. Like a pro who has done the act many times before, I brought my son down, placed him on top of the hood of my car, cradled his little head in my left arm, and placed my right middle and index fingers on his little chest. I pushed softly down on his chest and then gave two small puffs of air into his nose and mouth. I did it three times, and he suddenly began to spit up. I cleared his mouth and airway, and he began to cry as the ambulance got there. He was a sick little guy, having what they called febrile convulsions due to a sudden high fever. He spent the next couple of years on medication. Later on, Joanne explained to me what happened.

Now it's here, once again, that you will recognize the Hand of God. At 11:00 on the night prior to this happening, I was leaving to go to work, and Joanne was fast asleep in our room. She is a sound sleeper; I mean, when she's out, she hears nothing. In any event, I went into our son's room and checked on him. He was sleeping soundly. There was no hint of anything being wrong or about to go wrong. Within the next couple of hours,

Joanne was awakened by a voice telling her to "check the baby." She got up and found him turning blue and not breathing. She ran for the phone, and without knowing the phone number of the police department, she dialed the exact seven-digit number of the police department and requested help. Today, my son is a six-foot, 225-pound police SWAT sniper, married with three lovely daughters. Do you think God's divine intervention was at work here? That I would have given God the credit due him? Nope, not me. I continued on with my life, not missing a beat. However, this "happening" caused me to wonder. It brought back the angel experience from years before and stuff from Vietnam. The door was open, I had questions, and my quest for the truth began. It began slowly and would take me down many paths, but it began.

After what happened with my son, I started searching for the truth, the truth that is "humanity": why we exist, why things happen the way they do; in general, what was the point of us. Early on, my uncle introduced me to masonry. As a young boy, I had been a Boy Scout, which did have a positive influence on me—at first. My uncle got me involved with a group called Demolay, which, if I recall correctly, was sponsored by the Masons. I walked away from this organization; I was a loner and was uncomfortable in this group. Years later, my uncle spoke to me about becoming a Mason. I was interested, I was searching for answers, and the secrecy of the masons intrigued me. So a Mason I became. It suited me, as it was not a religious group, no "Bible thumpers," and they did good things. I spent some eighteen years in masonry. I paid my dues but participated very little. And I became a Shriner to boot. It gave me a respectability and was full of mystery, secrecy, and pageantry. I had a fancy Masonic ring and knew all the secret stuff. Besides, not everyone could be a Mason.

I was content, even though my outside life and activities were less than virtuous. I was also troubled by certain doctrines within Masonry; some things nagged at my psyche. I would question things, and questionable answers would be given. I never followed up. I accepted their answers and remained silent. By all standards, I was a good "brother" mason. This brotherhood filled a gap that neither the military nor the police department did. Masons always took care of each other. It was part of our pledge, our code, and it was expected.

I went forth in my life and career, obtaining a college degree in criminal law. As part of my search for "truth"—as I called it—I had for some time questioned who I really was. I was conflicted over this. I had an internal clash of idealism, things as they should be, in contrast to things as they were. I pondered these things more and more. Due to this discordance, which seemed to be growing within me, I minored in psychology at college, at a Catholic College no less. I found psychology to my liking, and I studied me. I made changes to my character as it pertained to my job as a police officer. I took community relations classes and began teaching and lecturing at schools. I spent five years teaching at a police academy and developed a course called Police Occupational Stress, which I will tell you from personal experience is PTSD. I felt I was finally coloring inside the lines of my life. I went from citizen complaints against me for brutality and misconduct to no complaints for brutality and very few for anything else.

Joanne and I had been blessed with a daughter along the way, and I had moved up the line financially at the police department. Joanne, who was an expert upholsterer and seamstress, started a sewing business out of our home, which became very successful. I was going to college and becoming savvy in the ways of human relationships. I dismantled my self-serving ego and replaced it with a more publicly acceptable image without giving up my self-esteem. It was a classic switch and bait: now you see it, now you don't. I was a quick study: my psych classes served my needs well. What was still going strong was my life in the street, my job, and my need for more and more adrenaline highs. The street is all-consuming; it's attractive, especially to nonbelievers. It's an action junkie's dream, and I moved in and out of the slime and shadows with ease. So what's missing here? God, of course. I never gave Him a moment's thought, which is a sinful condition, considering I received my bachelor's degree from a Catholic college, where religion was a required subject for graduation. (I got a B for doing extra credit.)

I was having an internal battle for my soul and clueless as to its origins, let alone what to do about it. While all this was going on—college, working, training, coaching junior high football, running the streets—I was also working part time as an undercover security officer, arresting shoplifters. I did this for fifteen years. I loved it and was very good at it. Anyway, I was employed by a large retail store and working with one of my partners from the PD (police department). We often worked security together, and on one such day, he told me the manager of the jewelry department—a woman of about fifty, small in stature, nicely dressed and groomed—had told him she was a witch, a white witch, in fact. He told me she wanted to meet me. Okay, I can hear you all now; it's not what you think. (It's more unbelievable than you think, so read on!) I asked why she wanted to meet me, and he didn't know. Well, I knew less about witches than I did God. The only witches I ever saw were in the *Wizard of Oz. Perhaps,* I thought, *as small as she is, maybe she's a munchkin.* In any event, I was curious and besides checking on jewelry, which was part of my job (it was a hot spot for snatch and grab guys), I went over and introduced myself. She didn't look like a witch (you know, no wart, broomstick, or anything you expect a witch to have). Me being me, I asked her right out, "Are you a witch? My buddy tells me you're a witch. Just what does that mean?" She promptly told me she was a white witch. "What's that?" I asked. She told me she was a "good" witch; in fact, she said she was a Christian witch. Please don't burn the book. It gets more bizarre.

Now, my life has been full of bizarre, so I wasn't shocked. In fact, oddly enough, I felt relaxed and unthreatened in her presence. I told her I had never met a witch and that I knew next to nothing of Christianity, but I didn't think they were compatible. I asked her what a white witch did. She began to explain there are white witches and black witches, and black witches are evil. They do very bad things and are in league with the devil. She was a white witch and worshipped God, did only good in the world, healed, and could see auras." I had no clue what "auras" were, so I asked. She said every person has an aura around their body, which is a luminous atmosphere of colors. She said the colors, their brightness, and intensity mean different things. I asked, "Do you see them now?"

"Oh, yes," she replied. "Everyone I see going by has one."

"Do I? Do you see one around me?" I asked.

"I do," she said.

She went on to tell me it was an unusual combination of colors and intensity. I was amazed. I didn't know if I should run as far as I could or knock her out. But my psychology studies dictated and directed my curiosity, and besides, I wasn't scared of her. I thought, *What does this lady want?* I asked her what all these colors meant. She told me they were very curious, special, and that she had a friend coming into town the following week. He was an author. And a warlock—a male witch—specifically a white warlock. Oh yes, it gets more interesting; hang onto your seats. She wanted yours truly to meet him, because he sees auras as well. Oh boy, can you even fathom what's going through my mind at that point?

The following week, my presence was requested at the jewelry department. On arrival, Ms. White Witch introduced me to Mr. White Warlock. He was a very distinguished-looking man of about seventy, with gray, neatly trimmed hair; of medium build; and dressed to the nines in a conservative suit. (I was observant—it's the cop in me, can you tell?) He was very nonthreatening; he looked and made you feel like he was any kid's well-to-do grandfather, or he owned the store. In any event, I was at ease in his presence. When introduced, he quickly offered his hand in greeting. I shook his hand firmly, and his grip was pleasantly firm—no weakness there. But he held onto my hand slightly longer than such a meeting might require. He looked directly into my eyes. His eyes were clear and soft, like a grandfather's might be. He smiled and told me how pleased he was to meet me. While exchanging niceties, I was very aware he had covered both our still-clasping right hands with his left hand. The only time I have ever experienced this form of greeting is when Masons cover their secret handshake or when elderly ladies patty-pat your hand as they hold it. We finally unclasped our hands and began a conversation of no particular importance. He was soft-spoken, articulate, and talked to me, not at me. He was not intimidated by me. This was something I have little experience with, because most everyone I go one on one with usually is intimidated by me. Intimidating people is not a characteristic I am proud of, but it is what it is, and according to my daughter, she lost a number of school friends after they met me. Anyway, we were talking when he turned to the White Witch and said something like, "You were so right. It's very unusual."

She smiled at him. "I told you it was."

Not being shy, without hesitation I asked, "Are you talking about me?"

He responded by apologizing and said, "Yes, I am, and you have an extremely unusual aura." I asked him to explain what all this aura stuff meant. He told me he believed in God and was a Christian. He had written nine books, ranging in subject matter from God, outer space, Christianity, life forms, and well, I won't belabor this subject. Then he told me, "Your aura indicates to me that God has a plan for you. He has something for you to do before you leave this world."

Of course, I asked the obvious question. "And what would it be that God wants me to do?"

His reply was matter of fact. "I don't know. That's within God's purview, but whatever it is, it's important." Well, I guess you can imagine what I was thinking. I was waiting for him to sell me his books or offer to read my palm. I don't know, maybe feel the bumps on my head. He did none of that. He politely broke off the conversation with his "having to be going," said good-bye and left. I blew the whole thing off as just two more bizarre people in the merry-go-round I called my life. I never saw either one of these two people again.

I'll bet you are happy we are beyond Oz and have stopped following the yellow brick road.

My life kept on keeping on. There was more to come for me as I walked through my world of the wild, weird, and the unexplainable. It's like falling down a rabbit hole and ending up in Wonderland with Alice.

The fact is, I was functioning as normally as I knew how. My home, wife, and kids were my sanctuary, my absolute security, where normal was, in fact, normal. All the while, I was still searching, looking for reasons, the how and why of it all. I never even shared this quest with my wife. The paths I was taking in my quest were often dark, ugly, and almost always dead ends. Sure, she was curious, asked questions, and wondered, but I kept her mostly at arm's length. I, in my way, was protecting her from what I saw, did, and knew. I worried it could harm her. I did, however, introduce her once to the underbelly of the streets: the subculture I worked in and knew. She wanted to know where I went and what I did. I knew she was concerned and felt left out, so I told her I was going to go-go bars and gay bars with my brother and other morality cops. I assured her we were not gay and that it was a bar owned by the "Prince of Queers," as he called himself. He allowed the morality guys to crash there, where no one would think to look for them. Plus, he never charged us for food and drinks. So my wife and I, and another couple made a night out of it and ended up at this bar. The owner was ecstatic that we would bring our wives to his club. Our wives were treated with great respect but were less than ecstatic. My wife never again wanted to know about the "neon slime world" I traveled in. Before passing judgment on me, keep in mind that 24-7, 365 days a year, there are men and women out there working to keep the slime in the swamp, and it's not easy. "Lie down with dogs, and you're bound to get fleas"—especially if you have little to no ethics or morals and live in the flesh without faith or grace in your life.

This world is of the flesh, God knows it, the Beast knows it, I know it, and you should know it. Keep in mind the only faith I had at that point was in myself, and I was struggling and working to keep from going totally under. I was being helped; I just didn't know it. God works in mysterious ways.

It was time to start putting one foot in front of the other and get away from witches and gays and slippery slopes into dark places where no one should be going. I'm sure you won't disagree that so far, the things I've written about might have little if anything to do with religion, God, Christianity, or Jesus. Please hang in there—it will become clear. (Remember, I told you to read between the lines, and things will start to develop, and the way will become clear.)

Now I will explain how my life moved in a direction that, once again, changed me forever physically, psychologically, and emotionally. Hang on: it's still bumpy, but it ends up smooth.

My career in law enforcement was long, varied, wild, and often dangerous. But though I had numerous injuries from ruptured disks, torn muscles, damaged knees, and more, nothing prepared me for what I would experience on a cold February night in 1986. (Note: my son's near-death incident as an infant also occurred on a cold February night, and I was born on a cold February night in 1948.) So, on a cold February night, I had already worked my 4:00 p.m. to midnight shift and then was "ordered" to work midnight to 8:00 a.m. (the graveyard shift). I was working a double: sixteen hours straight. I was not inclined to do so, as I was tired, cold, and ready to go home, but I was ordered to work. I was a good soldier, a warrior, and I loved the streets. So I'd give it 110 percent like always.

About 2:00 a.m., I received a "BOL" (be on the lookout) for a stolen car. The description of the car and the thief were given. I had been a street cop for some eighteen years and was very good at it. I knew all possible escape routes out of my city. I drove directly to the area escape route Mr. Bad Guy would most likely use. There he was, cruising along as if he owned the car. He looked right at me, and me at him, and the chase was on! Since it was February—the time of year when it warms during the day and then rains—by nightfall, all the roadways were covered with a two-inch sheet of ice. Well, bad guys don't care about stuff like road conditions. All they know is that they don't want to go to jail. So Mr. Bad Guy cuts his headlights and floors the vehicle with me in hot pursuit. We reached speeds of 80 miles per hour. I didn't want to exceed that for a number of very sound reasons; the least of which were two inches of ice. The bad guy could not shake me at 80 miles per hour, so he upped the ante by hitting speeds of 110 miles per hour, driving like he was possessed (more likely high). He bottomed out, busting stop signs, but his tactic worked, as he was leaving me behind. However, what I knew and he didn't was that he was rapidly approaching a three way T-intersection, and at his high rate of speed, he could not stop in time to make his turn. Mr. Bad Guy hit the intersection at about 100 miles per hour. The car dipped and then ran up onto the next piece of road like a roller coaster car. As he came to the stop sign and the need to make a decision to turn left or right, we both got a surprise! He hit the curb and went airborne—it was like watching the *Dukes of Hazzard*—reaching a height of some five feet. He crashed through the front picture window of a house, his speed propelling him through the living room wall and into the kitchen. Now, I wasn't going his speed; I had slowed down to about seventy miles per hour. I was well trained and experienced at high-speed driving, but I didn't calculate the huge pool of ice the dip in the road held, and I was braking as Mr. Bad Guy drove through the house. My car began fishtailing and was catapulted into the four-foot cement porch he had gone over. My car came to a sudden stop. My body did not. The force of the crash dislocated my right hip, and I became trapped in the wreckage. As I was vaulted back, the head of my right femur was driven into and through my pelvis. To make a long story short, I was in critical condition and spent the next two years recuperating. My career as a police officer, public safety firefighter, and EMT was over.

I ended up with a lot of time on my hands: a lot of time to reflect, to think, to ponder. But it would be another few years before my eyes would see and my ears would hear. Stay tuned … it's coming … still a few stumbling blocks to get over.

After recovering and learning to walk again (they had not replaced my hip at this point), I was mobile but limped noticeably and never returned to police work. My wife and I sold out and moved to a northern part of our state, far from the mean streets and slime of human degeneration I was used to. My new environment suited me. I had been so badly hurt and was so emotionally drained the seclusion, peace, and quiet had a healing effect on my psyche, and I thrived. I pondered many things in my life—past, present, and future. I got back to some things I used to enjoy, like reading. I went back to work, teaching at a high school and sold real estate in the summer. I met a lot of good people. There were reminders of my past life here and there, but they were minimal. My son returned from military service. My daughter moved near us. I was relaxed and enjoying my life.

I also reflected on my search for truth. A few years after moving north, I was pondering what it was several people I knew—a couple I knew personally and others through their books—had discovered. They knew "the truth," and the truth had made them strong, stable people who positively impacted others. My analysis found these people came from various backgrounds, were all well educated, and all had strength of character. They had one other thing in common: Christianity. They all gave credit to a man called Jesus Christ for everything in their lives. They all believed they were blessed. Think about it. With my past, the life I had lived, I was drawn to these individuals and studied them and read their books, I knew with certainty that I was led to do this. It opened my mind. I developed a "vision quest." I needed and was compelled to find out just what and who Christianity and Jesus were.

And so it began. I went from walking on the wild side to walking into religion, the Bible, and the Divine. I would spend two years studying the Bible and a number of Christian books. I had no idea where to start, so I asked my wife if she knew where a Christian bookstore might be. She did, and the next day I went to that store. Joanne must have thought, *Who is this guy, and what did you do with my husband?* There were dozens, if not hundreds of books at that Christian bookstore. I was in a quandary, but as had happened to me a few times in the past, a calm came upon me. I was at peace, and as I looked over the many books, I would be drawn to a particular book. I picked it up, somehow knowing it was a book I needed. I did this again and again, one book after another, and ended up leaving the Christian bookstore with several books on Christianity. I spent about $250.

I was elated! I was working my vision quest. My wife wasn't so sure, as this was a bit outside the box for me. But as always, she supported and encouraged me. I am blessed because of her. My two-year self-study course began. Like everything I ever did, I put 110 percent into my studies. It was not easy. I often got very confused, going from reference book to Bible, and Bible back to reference book. Yet, in time, in the quiet of my northern setting, things started to come to life. I slowly began to understand Christianity, at least fundamentally. But near the end of my two-year study program, I reached an impasse. I couldn't put Christianity in perspective. It was like a jigsaw puzzle. I had the outside borders in place and 98 percent of the puzzle complete, but that last 2 percent eluded me. Then it happened. I was studying in bed late one night; I often studied late into the night. My wife was fast asleep next to me. I had Christian texts open all over me and the bed. Ink pens, yellow highlighters, notepads: yes, I was deep into trying to get that puzzle to come together. As often happened, I fell asleep while studying. Late in the early morning hours, I woke up. I woke up, and the Holy Spirit had come upon me. I finally fully understood that which I had been seeking for so many years: truth. And the truth wasChristianity. The truth was crystal clear to me. Jesus Christ is the way to truth, and at that moment, I was born again. I accepted Jesus as my personal savior; I believed, fully accepted, and was very clear on the fact Jesus died for my sins. My eyes were opened and clear, my ears could hear, and it was clear. I cannot tell you how wonderful it was, there in the quiet of my sanctuary. I woke my wife to share my elation, and she was glad for me. What a fantastic blessing I received that night, and I have never looked back.

"Carpe diem, life is short, seize the day, for the wolves are at the door." The very foundation of Christianity is being shaken and could collapse. Now is truly the time for Christians to stay the course, talk the talk, and walk the walk. Business as usual for Christians just isn't going to save Christianity today. I fear these things, because I have been in the shadow of the beast, where all paths of the flesh lead to darkness, misery, and eventually destruction. My wife and I moved quickly after I was born again and became a Christian. We went to several churches where we lived, looking for a Bible-believing church. I knew when we found it, we would know it. We spent a number of months searching for a church and finally entered one and instantly felt at home. We settled into our new home church and were blessed.

In about 1996, we relocated to be closer to our grandchildren and settled in a farm area an hour from our children. A couple years after we relocated, I required surgery on my left knee to repair damage from an injury. It was routine surgery; not to worry, right. That's the story of my life as a patient in hospitals: "not to worry." I reported to a local hospital, had outpatient surgery, and home I went. Within about four days, the not to worry procedure turned my leg fire engine red. I am the first to admit I'm not the smartest guy around, but fire engine red, well, I just knew that wasn't okay. Not to mention my leg was hot to the touch. To the emergency room I went. The nurse took one look, and the next thing I knew, I was in a hospital bed, hooked up to IV drip bags. I surveyed my situation and found my surroundings to be adequate, if not pleasant, and thought I could get a lot of reading done, as I had brought a couple of books, including my Bible.

However, tranquility was not in my future. I shared a room with another patient, and he was, from outward appearances, a little person (a dwarf). He was grossly disfigured: his body was deformed to the point that most people wanted to divert their gaze. And many people did exactly that and quickly moved on. His speech could not be understood, but he would yell constantly. This went on night and day, with short periods of quiet. This man, if not in physical pain, was most certainly in emotional pain. As annoying as his constant yelling was, I found myself saddened at his condition. I experienced a heavy-heartedness I was unaccustomed to and found myself, oddly enough, accepting this man, not as an annoyance to be rid of, but as a person, a human being who should be shown care and concern, if not to be understood. I was asked more than once by hospital staff if I wanted to be moved to another room, and I said no. I explained my roommate could not help himself, and his pain and suffering were sorrowful to me. It was something that I would adapt to and overcome.

So it was that I settled into my recovery. I prayed for my roommate and read my books, including my Bible. One time as I was reading my Bible, my surgeon came into the room. He was a very pleasant guy and greeted me almost like a friend. He made note of my roommate's vocalizations and told me he could get me moved to another room. I declined his offer, telling him it was not necessary. The poor guy could not help it and did not bother me. He lauded me for that and then noticed and commented that I was reading the Bible. I told him I was a Christian and read not only the Bible but other Christian books, as I was still studying and learning more about my faith. He identified himself and his wife as Christians. He completed his exam of my leg, explaining it was not going as well as he had hoped. The infection was very bad, and it was a wait-and-see situation. There was a possibility I could lose my leg to the infection. I was concerned for my leg, and I prayed for my health and welfare. And I prayed for my roommate.

The following day, my surgeon came back into my room with a book. He told me that while at dinner with his wife, he told her about me and my roommate, that I was a Christian, and so on. According to him, his wife was so moved by what he told her that she went right out and bought a book for me. The good doctor told me she felt certain, based on the story her husband told her, I needed to read this book. To say the least, I was speechless, a trait I do not normally possess. He handed me the book and continued on his way. The book was by Charles R. Swindoll, an author I did not know at the time but who would become my favorite Christian author. It was titled *David: A Man of Passion and Destiny.* It is my opinion that Swindoll is the finest Christian writer of our time. I was already involved with reading three other books, so I put this book aside to take with me when I was released from the hospital. The next morning, my leg had taken a turn for the better and was healing. The following day, the troublesome infection was gone. Go figure: a blessed man? I'm going with yes!

I was discharged from the hospital, went home, and placed the book about David on the nightstand next to my bed, under a stack of other books I was reading or wanted to get to in due course. *David,* the book, passed into my memory. With that, we will move on, but I will return to *David: A Man of Passion and Destiny* later.

I settled back in the routine of life. Joanne and I were active in our church, and I was striving to be the best Christian I could be. This is not to say I did not backslide on occasion, because, of course, I did, and do. Now, I am quick to repent and ask the Lord for forgiveness. I never hesitate to dispel the beast (Devil) when he creeps into my life, my thoughts, my psyche—and he does try but not as often as he once did. When I sense his presence, I immediately rebuke him and invoke the name of Jesus by ordering the devil to "get behind me beast/devil and stay there in Jesus' name." This works, and the devil lets me be. Jesus is within me, I believe by faith alone and grace alone, and this will not change for me. It's eternal.

So on went my life, problems and all. Oh yes, Christians have problems. We stumble, we fall, we persevere. Carry on I did. Since moving closer to my children and grandchildren, I have dislocated my hip six times. It is very unnerving to do so. It's painful and requires surgery to put the hip back into the socket. I had a hip replacement, and that began my six various trips to the emergency room followed by surgery. So I know a lot about hospitals, pain, and recovering. On one such trip to the emergency room and subsequent surgery, I was thrust into a frightening nightmare of events that would end with the Lord blessing me once again. I was being prepared for surgery, and the anesthetist was having trouble inserting a tube down my throat. In his effort to insert the tube, he ruptured my esophagus, which swelled and closed off my ability to breathe. Reportedly, I stopped breathing, and my heart stopped beating. Routine surgery turned into CPR, as a special device needed to open my airway was missing from the surgical room. Someone had performed manual CPR for six minutes. One thing led to another, the missing device was located, and I was brought back to breathing on a respirator.

My wife and children had been escorted into a private room, where they were informed I had stopped breathing for some six minutes, with no heartbeat, and my prognosis was not good. Joanne, my son, and daughter were told that considering the time I had with no substantial oxygen to my brain, it was probable I would be in a vegetative state, wherein I would need constant care for the rest of my life. My family was told they might consider placing me in a long-term facility that could deal with someone in my condition. This information scared my family to their core.

The fact is I came out of surgery, eventually recovered, and experienced no adverse physical effects. I did, however, suffer from deep emotional trauma. On returning home,

I did not *feel* normal; nothing hurt physically, yet I felt injured. I quietly tried to return to a normal routine, but I couldn't. My mind was preoccupied with feelings of disassociation. I felt lost, unwell, wrong. These feelings grew stronger by the day, and I didn't care if I lived or died. I began to argue with God as I tried to pray for His help. My wife and I grew angry with each other and distant. Month after month, I slipped deeper into a dark place. I was hostile, argumentative, and wanted no one around me. For days at a time, I went nowhere. Refusing to seek professional help, I suffered alone, trapped in the deep, dark hole that was my mind. All this time, God and I were "arm wrestling." "Just take me, Lord. Why make me suffer?" I would argue.

So it went for almost a year. Then one day, Joanne, who was at her wits end with me, left to visit our grandchildren for a couple days. I was glad, because I liked suffering alone. By mid-afternoon, I was very depressed and engaged God in conversation. I spoke openly and with anger. "Take me, God, end my miserable life, but don't let me languish one more day like this." Now hear me folks, when arm wrestling or arguing with God, or whatever you might call it, the fact is God always wins. And if you are in an outraged or angry state of mind (which I don't recommend), you can expect God to rebuke you. Rebuke me He did. What I am about to tell you, I will paraphrase God's message in my words. He said to me, "Enough! Get up off your butt, pick up the book *David,* given to you some years prior, and read it! Listen to me now!" When

God speaks, you listen, and I did. I immediately got up and went to my bedroom, where you will recall I buried the book of *David* under other books on the nightstand next to my bed. The book was where I had left it. I cleaned the dust off its cover and returned to the comfort of my chair. I found myself surprisingly at peace with myself for the first time in many months. Having died and been brought back, for me, can only be explained as follows: you don't come back whole. You come back in pieces; your soul is in pieces. And no matter how hard I tried, I could not bring the pieces together to make me whole, to make me, me.

So, when I sat back down in my chair, I opened *David: A Man of Passion and Destiny,* by the author I did not know, and read it from cover to cover. When I awoke the next morning, the darkness that had been with me for so many months was gone, and I was me once again. I was whole, at ease, and at peace with not only myself but everything around me. Divine intervention. Yes, that's exactly what it was, and once again, God blessed me. No one is more surprised than I every time God touches my life with His Grace. Glory be to God who loves us and forgives sins, shortcomings, backslidings, self-pitying behaviors, and all. I never wish to experience that intensity of darkness again.

I do believe God allows such adversity in our life so we might become stronger. As steel is hardened in fire and comes out stronger, so it is that we (in the flesh) as Christians encounter any number of difficulties in our lives. Through such adversities, we suffer its intensity, its fire if you will, and we are made better, stronger in our souls. "That which doesn't kill you, will make you stronger"—a truism I live by, having gone through some eight periods of rehabilitation from traumatic injuries and the many surgeries I have had.

My body and soul are seared from adversities, and I have physical pain every waking hour. But I am a blessed man. God, the Holy Spirit, and my Lord Jesus Christ never gave up on me. The Trinity is with me always, and I endeavored to persevere in my search for truth. I found the truth in Christ in His Word, and I now will forever walk in His light. When God is most near to me, and I need him the most, I always experience a quietness, a silence that puts me into a calmness that is soothing, and I think clearly and am unafraid. One such moment occurred when I was driving my classic 1960 Ford tractor across a makeshift wooden bridge in the middle of my eighty-acre woodlot. I was pulling a brush hog to a wildlife field I had planted and was in the process of crossing the bridge that spanned a twelve-foot deep ditch. I heard the boards on the bridge crack, and the left side of the bridge failed. Down I went, with the tractor ending upside down on top of me. I was trapped between the ground and rear axle and tires of the tractor at the bottom of the ditch. By God's grace, the ditch was not full of water, but it was slightly muddy. I was slowly being crushed and had difficulty breathing. My situation was dire, and I knew death was imminent. I attempted to yell for help, as a friend of mine had gone ahead of me to the field. My words came out with difficulty, as it was hard to breathe let alone yell. My friend later stated he did not hear anything he could identify but thought he heard something. When I did not show up at his location, he came looking for me. By the time my friend found me, I was fading fast, and I advised my friend I was dying. He wanted to go for help, because he couldn't get me out from under the tractor. I told him I would be dead by the time he returned with help. I was getting light-headed when a calm came upon me. It got quiet and serene. My friend was kneeling next to me, and I told him I was going to die and to tell Joanne I loved her. My friend became very animated, excitedly stating, "You're not going to die! I won't let you!" He jumped up and began looking for something he could use to get me out. My friend is not a large man, and he is older than I, but he is a former marine (warriors and patriots, well, we just adapt and overcome). Quickly, he found a sturdy length of wood and using leverage under the bell housing of the tractor, he stood on the end of the wood and bounced up and down. In doing so, he got the tractor to lift just a small amount and with the small amount of mud under me, like an earthworm, I was able to slither my body forward. It took several minutes, but I was able to free myself. Once again, I escaped death, God was with me, blessed me once again, and although deeply bruised and scuffed up, I was not seriously injured.

I feel and believe I am truly a blessed man. God's grace is upon me as I go through life, and He has always been there. I was lost, blind, and deaf for so long, and now I am found, I see clearly, and I hear God's word. I feel strongly about God's desire for us to spread the Gospel to others. We plant the seed and move on, letting the Holy Spirit take over. I believe in serving others, and my life has always been about service. I have mentored kids and served my country, state, and community. I have physically and emotionally given much. I regret none of it, with the exception of the time lost in my life not knowing Christ.

The Kingdom of God is a kingdom of paradox where,
through the ugly defeat of a cross, a Holy God
is utterly glorified. Victory comes through
defeat; healing through brokenness;
finding self through losing self.

Chuck Colson

Chapter VI
Carpe Diem … Seize the Day

Life is short; seize the day. If you are already a devoted Christian, walking His walk and talking His talk, you need to stay the course. Sure, times can be tough; adversity will find its way into your life. You might backslide from time to time, but remember, Christ died for you. His blood was shed for you and washed away your sins. These facts will never change. He will never forsake you. Those of you who are nonbelievers, who, like me, are in search of eternal truth, need look no farther than the Holy Bible. It contains everything you need to know about the truth, the human condition, life in general, and all other questions you will have. When I was attending a Catholic college and had religion class, I was a nonbeliever. And because of that, I found the study of Christianity very difficult. I also studied Judaism and Islam and found them easier to follow than Christianity.

Being a Christian and walking the path of Christianity here on earth is not easy. The influences of living "in the flesh" are very strong and often attractive. The flesh is weak, and sin often makes the flesh feel good and happy; it is addictive. The path of living in the flesh leads only to self-destruction. You will become lost, you will desire more, and you will sin exceedingly. It can and will destroy you and all you love (family, friends, and, most important, your soul.) So I implore you, it's never too late to pick up a Bible, walk into a Bible-believing church, go to a Christian bookstore, or just begin to pray. I can't say enough about prayer. Do it, wherever you are, whenever you feel the need. Talk to your Father in Heaven. He is listening. Talk to Him like you would a good friend. He is listening. You should know, however, that when our Father grants prayers, He will often give you what you need, not necessarily what you want.

Whenever you can, say the prayer given to us by God: the Our Father. You should know the rest of it. Say it now; it is His gift to us. I have done my duty to God in this chapter and have planted the seed. It is my hope you, the readers, have opened your hearts and minds so that seed will grow strong, and the Holy Spirit will come to you to fertilize the seed, that you will know God's word, and that your soul will be saved in Jesus' name through His shed blood. Peace be with you always.

*Standing for right when it is unpopular
Is a true test of moral character.*

Margaret Chase Smith

*Speak up for those who cannot speak up for
themselves, for the rights of all who are destitute.*

Proverbs 31:8 NIV

*To be right with God has often meant
to be in trouble with men.*

A. W. Toz

Chapter VII

Veritas Ae'quitas

My entire life I have wanted and searched for truth and justice. I am a warrior patriot and lived for a long time in the flesh, without benefit of Jesus in my life. In my search for justice, I was unaware that it was as close to me as the Holy Bible. So it was I followed many paths that ended in disappointment for me and left me spiritually empty inside. Justice, truth, right, wrong, and reasoning all were contradictions I struggled with. Law, ethics, and morality did not go hand in hand. What ought to be was not always what was. For example, twice in my career as a police officer, I was placed in a situation where a man's life was at stake, depending on what he or I did. The first incident involved a search for a man with a gun, who had left his home and was going to his wife's place of employment to kill her. He was reported to be armed and dangerous. I drove to her place of employment, where I saw the suspect in his car. I pulled in front of him, exited my car, and confronted him at gunpoint. I ordered him to exit his car, hands raised. He sat, staring at me. He was a tough-looking man. I could tell he was contemplating his next move. I was about twenty yards from him; my pistol was pointed directly at him. He slowly opened his car door and stepped out. He did not surrender himself, raise his arms, or say a word. He reached into the backseat and pulled out a shotgun. It is at this point many police officers might have taken his life. I ordered him to drop his weapon. He turned and stared at me. His expression showed no emotion, but again, I felt he was deciding what he would do next. I told him to drop the weapon or I would shoot him. I knew that unless he pulled the shotgun out of the vehicle and pointed it at me, I was not going to shoot him. You see, I made a conscious, informed decision not to take this man's life, because I had grown up around guns and hunting, and my first shotgun was a single-barrel gun that had to be cocked before it could be fired. The man before me, a trigger pull away from dying, was holding such a shotgun, and it was not cocked. After a few minutes of contemplation, the man dropped the shotgun and was taken into custody.

Officers from the jurisdiction that put out the original alert witnessed the incident. They not only questioned the way I handled this situation but filed an official report with my department's chief of police. I found myself explaining my decision not to kill this man. I told him my reasoning as I have told it here. He told me the other cops wanted me fired for cowardice. I told my chief I had no problem taking the shot if it became necessary, but it did not. Had I done so, it would have been tantamount to intentional murder. I informed the chief I was not a murderer. Having to kill in the line of duty in defense of myself or someone else, I would do, but I would not commit murder. The chief agreed, and that was that.

Until the next time, which occurred a few years later. I once again found myself on routine patrol and heard a call go out that was on the border of my jurisdiction and a sister city's jurisdiction. A man had reportedly fired shots inside a bar full of patrons. He was very drunk, was wearing a suit, and had left the scene. I was close to the bar and rolled up just as the described man stumbled in front of my car and across a seven-lane highway. I exited my car and yelled at him to stop. He turned to face me. I was only about thirty feet away from him. He had all the characteristics of someone who was drunk. His clothing was in disarray, his hair was mussed up, his tie was askew, and he was speaking incoherently. I immediately noticed the gun tucked in the front of his trousers. He was stumbling about, speaking words I couldn't make out, so I doubt he understood my orders to put his hands in the air. In any event, he reached down and took hold of the gun with his right hand. I yelled at him not to pull out the gun, or I would shoot him. I had my gun pointed directly at his chest; he was moments from being shot dead. But I was in command. I had dealt with many dangerous drunken people, and his body language did not exhibit a desire or intent to engage me in hostile action of any kind. He did not exhibit the "mean drunk syndrome," and I did not fear him. In most cases, what he did next would have cost him his life if another officer had encountered the man. But I knew instinctively I was not in danger, and I was not going to take that man's life. He pulled out the gun, but he never raised it at me. Had he done so, I would have shot him. Instead, he opened the cylinder of the revolver and emptied the remaining shells onto the street. He was taken into custody without incident.

Was it a judgment call, cowardice on my part, or the Hand of God? You decide. There is no doubt in my mind. In any case, because of witnesses, I once again had to explain my actions to my chief. Why did I not shoot this guy when he put his hand on his gun or when he pulled it out? How do I explain what I did? Oh, God's hand was in charge, it was a blessing, the grace of God dictated my actions. That is exactly how I would explain my actions today, as a true Christian. But remember, I was not a Christian while on the police force. Christianity was still in my distant future. So I did a fast two-step and explained myself. Once again, my chief agreed, and I was exonerated. I was never given a citation for outstanding police work for not killing these two men. I was never praised for my actions. To this day, I have difficulty wrapping my mind around how I could save the lives of two human beings and have my decisions and actions in doing so scrutinized as they were. Not that I needed it, but an attaboy would have been nice. So doing what's right was not, according to some standards, the right thing to do. Such is life in the flesh. It's the way things are, the way things get done, especially when God is left out of the process. When morals, ethics, and integrity are lacking in the human condition of processing information and making decisions, any number of things from bad to sinful to evil can happen.

My walk through life has put me in many situations where I had difficulty grasping the meaning of it all in terms of life as a human being. During the nightmare that was the infamous Tet Offensive of 1968, I had an occasion to be assisting in base camp at our MASH unit. Two ARVAN (South Vietnamese soldiers) arrived, carrying a small girl about five years old. A helicopter had been shot down, and it crashed into the village. This child was in harm's way. She was a beautiful child: long, dark hair; almond-shaped, dark brown eyes. She stared at me like a fawn caught in a car's headlights. She was not crying or talking. When they handed her to me, I saw her right arm was missing at the shoulder; it had been blown completely off. She was in shock, and I handed her to one of the doctors. She was immediately medevaced from our location to a hospital in Saigon that could handle such a severe wound. She was alive when they took her to the helicopter. To this day, I have wondered if she survived. This has haunted my memory ever since it happened. That child's eyes are with me always. I have shed numerous tears for her sake. The why—the reasoning—eludes me. As a Christian, I now understand and accept God's will. Bad things happen to good people, children, the innocent, believers, and nonbelievers alike.

They happen all the time. We live in the flesh; we are of flesh and blood, where things occur often by accident or out of one's control. Certainly, a child losing her arm to a crashing helicopter was not by design. We can ponder such things until our very souls cry out for it to stop, and yet we know that living here on earth in the flesh means such things will continue.

Only through our understanding and acceptance of God's truth can we find a way to accept those things over which we have no control. Prayer, study of God's word, and faith will soothe the soul and bring comfort to your heart. Do not forsake these things, as they are gifts from God and will help you endure until you are with Our Father in Heaven. I pray often, but probably not as much as I need to, and I'm forever working on that. In fact, I have a bumper sticker that reads, "I pray, get used to it." It's my way to let nonbelievers know that what they think or don't think is of little concern to me when it comes to Christianity and where and how I practice it. I've taken a stand. The line in the sand has been drawn, and I choose Jesus and Christianity as a way of life. Life is fleeting; it is ever so precious and can be snuffed out in the blink of an eye. I have seen it; I have had people die in front of my eyes. I am talking with them one second, and the next, they are gone. The human being who was is gone, that which felt pain or happiness, that which loved and was loved, felt anger, joy, or any one of the many emotions human beings experience is gone.

Gone where? I've had to ponder that as a nonbeliever.

It was not easy, I will tell you that. So it was late in my career as a police officer (prior to my life-changing, near-fatal car crash) when I had to deal with a mind-disturbing situation. It was Christmas Eve day, and I was required to attend the autopsy of a middle-aged man I had found deceased in his home, where he had been wrapping Christmas gifts. Because of his age and the circumstances surrounding his sudden death, an autopsy was done to rule out foul play. In fact, I witnessed a second autopsy that day. The only good thing that day was that I did not have to watch a third one. The only people in the room were the coroner and me—and the deceased, of course. The coroner was an older, experienced medical examiner, who had done hundreds, if not thousands, of autopsies. He had seen it all. I was no stranger to death myself, so I did not pay attention to the levity shown by the coroner. There was nothing solemn or reverent about the proceedings. It was just routine, as displayed by the skillfulness of the good doctor as he went about the business of determining cause of death. He would lightheartedly make a joke or display humor, a trait not uncommon to police officers and other professionals who deal with human tragedy. It is a way of protecting oneself from emotional distress at doing and seeing horrible things.

I was in a more somber mood, conflicted between life, death, the whys, the wherefores. There was disharmony between these ideas in my thoughts, to say nothing about it being Christmas Eve, and I did not want to be there, watching one human being dissecting another. I then had to go home to Christmas Eve dinner with my wife and children, where it was a certainty they would want to know what I did that day at work. I would fabricate a story and tell them how quiet and routine it was. Sometimes, a story is necessary and serves a good purpose when the harsh reality of the truth might be harmful. I had all this to think about, and I would question my career choice and why anyone would do the jobs that the coroner and I chose to do. Do it I did, and I did it efficiently, if not well. I was not only highly decorated while in Vietnam, but I was at the time of my career-ending accident the highest decorated officer on the police department. I can imagine how much that means to you, but it means even less to me. What did mean something to me and was worth more than all the citations and commendations I have ever received came from a grieving mother of a little boy killed in an auto accident. This little boy was killed on a sun-filled summer day on the curbside of a residential street. He was five years old and had been to a candy store with two siblings and was on his way home when a drunk driver hit him. When I arrived at the scene, I found the drunk, slobbering over the boy's lifeless body at the edge of the roadway. I pushed the drunk aside, got on the ground, and began CPR. (By this time in my career, I was a trained EMT). The child was not breathing, but the CPR worked, and his breathing returned. He did not regain consciousness and, sadly, never would. That little boy died three days later.

A week after his death, I was standing in the squad room of my police station when there was a knock at the back door. I answered it and spoke to a woman who identified herself as the little boy's mom. She asked if I was the officer who helped her son, and I told her I was. She took hold of me, kissed my cheek, and said she just wanted to thank me for giving her three last days with her son to say good-bye to him. She cried as she walked away, and as she closed the door behind her, I could not hold on any longer. As the vision of that little boy, lying in the street, bleeding and with a small bag of candy strewn around him, filled my memory, I found refuge in a private room and cried. That mother's kiss and hug for what I tried to do but failed is with me always.

It was what it was. I did my work as well as I could. I gave my all—almost my life, not to mention three body parts. I loved what I did; nothing gave me more pleasure than putting a person who did bad things in jail and holding him or her accountable for what had been done. It's who I was, not just what I did. So judge me if you will, but I do not regret my whole life or many of the things I've had to do. What I do wish is that I had found Jesus Christ earlier in my life, that I had not been physically hurt so often or so badly, and I that my psyche—my soul—was not scarred by what I've seen, heard, known, and done.

I have been a sinner. I have sinned exceedingly before God. I am, to the very essence of my soul, sorry for and repent of my sins against God and my family of Christian brothers and sisters. I walk with Christ now. He lights my way. I will never look back to what I was. Yes, I backslide from time to time. I stumble and fall, but my Lord and Savior Jesus Christ is always there. The outstretched Hand of God lifts me and sets my feet firmly on the path of righteousness. Praise be to God.

*And ye shall know the truth,
and the truth shall make you free.*

John 8:32 KJV

Conclusion

I would like to take credit for this book, but the fact is it belongs to God. Oh, it's my physical life that I wrote about and my words—as lacking in elegance as they were. But it was God who inspired me to set pen to paper. It was God who moved me to tell my story. I just didn't wake up and decide to write about my life. God's influence stirred me to action. This little book is God's. It's about Him. Sure, I'm in it, my life is exposed, but God used me as His canvas, and every incident in the book is His brushstroke on the canvas of my life. I hope it conveys God's message that sinfulness and nonbelief can be overcome. It is never too late to come to God through Jesus Christ and be born again by accepting Jesus as your personal savior. I put pen to paper per God's instructions to spread His message; to plant a seed in those who read these words and are inclined to open the door to the Holy Spirit and hear God calling to them. Glory be to God. To God all the glory be given.

You might have noticed that I used very few names in my writing. I identified no one except for Joanne, my wife, and I identified no states, cities, or myself. This was by design. The one exception is Charles R.

Swindoll, a gifted Christian writer whose book *David: A Man of Passion and Destiny* was a gift to me from God. In it, I found comfort. This writing is about God—no one else, no place, or thing. The focus is to be on God, Jesus, the Holy Spirit. I seek no fame or fortune. I am not a theologian, a professional minister, teacher, or writer. I am not a scholar of the Bible; I cannot quote scripture by chapter and verse, nor can I intelligently discuss religious doctrines to any great degree. But by living my life to the fullest, by seeking truth, and by questioning and listening to God when He speaks to me, I have a unique understanding of my overall connection to God. I do not claim to be the only person to have the feelings, thoughts, and experiences I've had. I am certain there are many people who have had their lives changed, have been born again out of worse experiences than mine, or have been touched by God's hand in more ways than He has touched me. I am doing the will of God the way He wishes me to do it. I do not look for anyone's confirmation or earthly blessings. Laude me not, for my ego does not require it. My Lord called to me, I answered His call, and this book was written. If you wish to do something, please pray. Pray for me and my family, pray for peace on earth, pray for peace in Israel, and pray for yourself. Pray the Lord's Prayer, the prayer given to us by our Father in Heaven. I thank you, my wife thanks you, and my son, daughter, and grandchildren thank you.

Note: Though I cannot recite scripture by chapter and verse, I do have my favorites:

Psalm 23:4
Matthew 5:10–12
Proverbs 22:6
John 3:16
Matthew 12:36–37
Romans 1:16

God's infallible words—His message—are breathed into the prophets/scribes who wrote them. There are many more in the Holy Bible. It is full of wisdom. Please read not only those I have listed but the Bible in its entirety. It will do your heart good, and you will feel peace within your soul. Peace of our Lord Jesus Christ be with you always.

tishimself
In God's Service

Special Tribute

I would be remiss if I did not pay tribute to the many thousands of men and women who, through their selfless service to others, have been wounded physically, emotionally, or completely by putting themselves in harm's way. Many of these individuals don't see themselves as in harm's way. These special people on the front line—where the human condition of pain, suffering, violence, hostility, disease, injury, sickness, mental and emotional distress, and death—are what they experience daily. These conditions are the stages upon which they ply their trades. They give of themselves every day. They are soldiers, fighter pilots, police officers, medics, firefighters, emergency room doctors and nurses, caregivers, and others. They can, and many do, suffer visible and invisible wounds. I am talking about posttraumatic stress disorder (PTSD), a condition many medical professionals will gladly attempt to define for you. However, I believe people who deal with the human condition at its worst, if they are caring and giving often, experience and suffer from scarring of their souls.

The essence of who we are, that which makes us well, us, is our soul, and many of us have various degrees of scarring on our souls, depending on our life experiences. In any event, that's how I see it, and I just felt the need to pay tribute to those of us who give of ourselves in service to all. Thank you, and God be with you always.

tishimself
In Service to God

About the Author

The the author at the time of this writing is sixty-three years old. After high school, he served in Vietnam with the First Infantry Division and was awarded a Purple Heart, a Bronze Star, and two Army Commendation Medals, among others. The author has a bachelor's degree in criminal law. He spent twenty-five years as a public safety officer/firefighter and ten years as an EMT. He has taught elementary through high school, including five years as a police academy instructor, and has mentored many kids. He has worked at and managed a youth center for juvenile delinquent boys, overseeing the daily operations of some forty employees and thirty-six boys. The author is 100 percent disabled through the US Army and 100 percent disabled through injuries he incurred as a police officer. He has two children. His son is a veteran of the US Coast Guard and is a SWAT sniper in a large, urban police agency. He is married with three lovely daughters. The author's daughter is a lawyer serving, the needs of the elderly and veterans. She has two sons. The author himself graduated with honors from a private Catholic College with a B.A. in Criminal Law. Unable to complete his Master's degree due to near fatal injuries, while working as a police officer/public safety officer, the author was retired. After retiring, the author and his wife of forty-three years reside in quiet anonymity, where they practice Christianity and enjoy the serenity of their farm and five grandchildren. The author enjoys hunting, riding his Harley Davidson motorcycle, making crafts, scrapbooking, and reading.

Contact Me
Motivational Speaker

If you would like to have me as a motivational speaker for your youth group, school, parents, or church groups, I am available to mentor.

Please e-mail your name and a contact number to cwtishimself@gmail.com.

In God's Service

Mr Charles G Woods
6880 Legg Rd
Kingston MI 48741-9717

CPSIA information can be obtained at www.ICGtesting.com
Printed in the USA
BVOW041622310512

291490BV00001B/1/P

9 781462 716968